MARTHA MIER'S
FAVORITE SOLOS
10 OF HER ORIGINAL PIANO SOLOS

MW00637161

FOREWORD

Each year Alfred publishes a variety of sheet music solos for students at various levels. Teachers and students use them for recitals, auditions, festivals, or just to have fun. Many of these become student favorites, and teachers continue to teach them through the years.

Just as teachers and students have their own preferences, the composers who write these solos also have their own personal favorites. For the Composer's Choice series, the editors at Alfred asked each composer to choose his or her best-loved sheet music solos that had been published through the years and compile them into graded collections for students. They were asked to reflect upon when they had written the pieces and see if the music evoked strong feelings or conjured up treasured memories. In addition, they considered the inspiration behind the pieces, students who had studied the music, or comments that they had received from teachers about the solos.

As a result of this process, Alfred is pleased to introduce Martha Mier's *Favorite Solos*, Book 1, a collection of ten early elementary to elementary solos for students of all ages. Students, teachers and audiences will enjoy the variety of styles, sounds and moods of this music. We feel sure that Martha's *Favorite Solos* will quickly become your favorites, too. Enjoy!

CONTENTS

Alfred

2

The Chocolate Song

Martha Mier

Happily

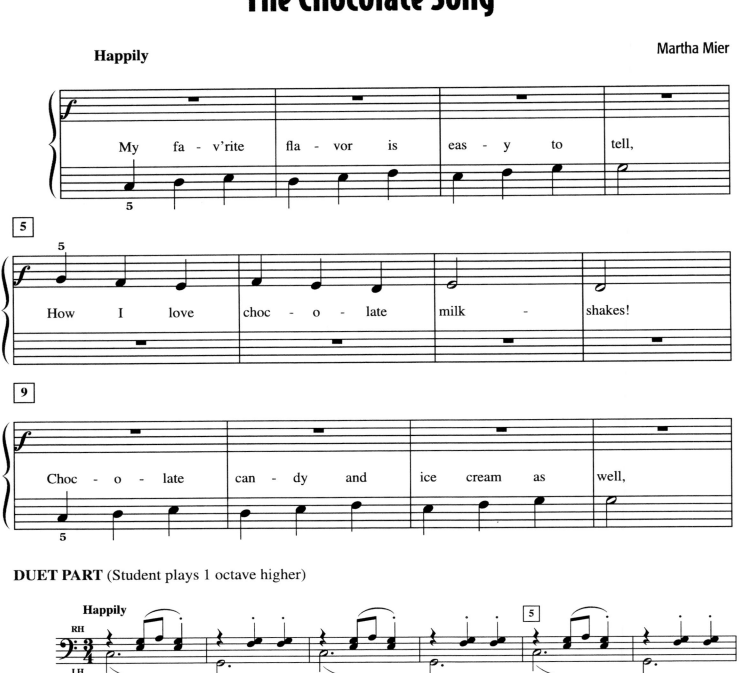

My fa - v'rite fla - vor is eas - y to tell,

How I love choc - o - late milk - shakes!

Choc - o - late can - dy and ice cream as well,

DUET PART (Student plays 1 octave higher)

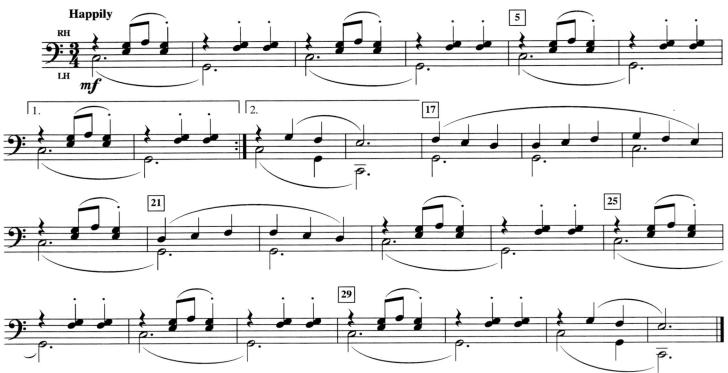

Happily

13

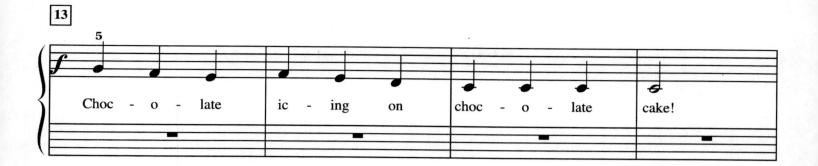

Choc - o - late ic - ing on choc - o - late cake!

17

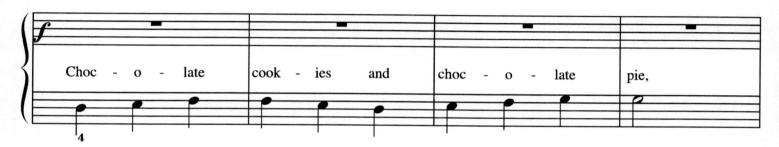

Choc - o - late cook - ies and choc - o - late pie,

21

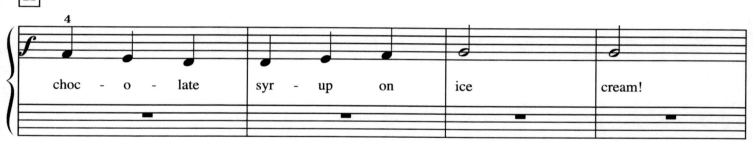

choc - o - late syr - up on ice cream!

25

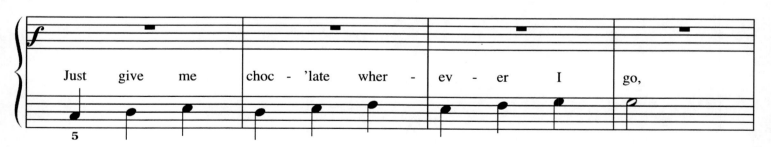

Just give me choc - 'late wher - ev - er I go,

29

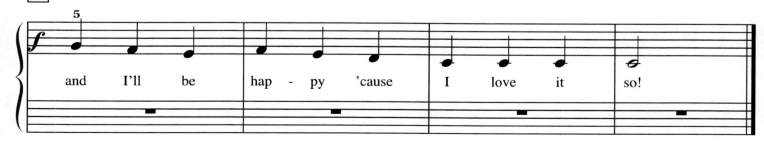

and I'll be hap - py 'cause I love it so!

Medieval Castle

Martha Mier

DUET PART (Student plays 1 octave higher)

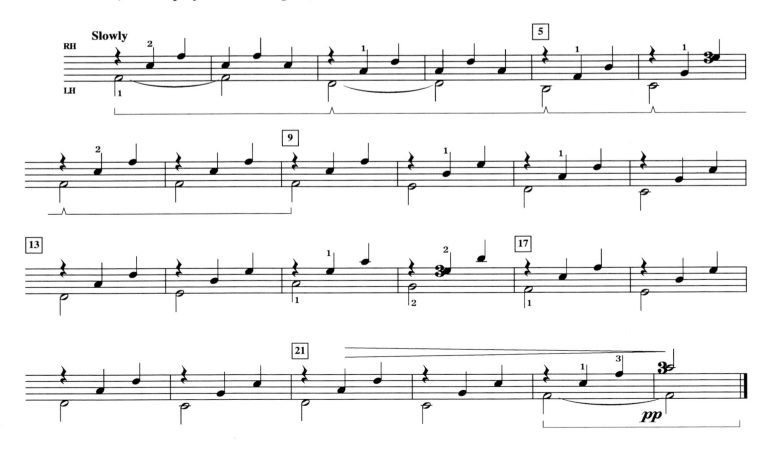

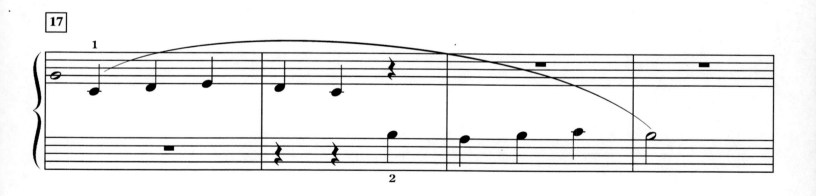

Nothin' to Do Blues

Martha Mier

Moderately slow

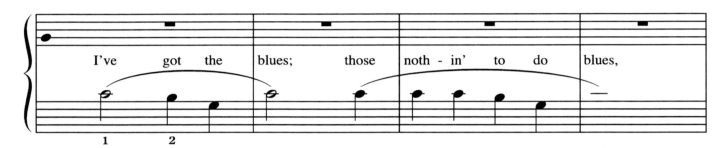

I've got the blues; those noth - in' to do blues,

DUET PART (Student plays 1 octave higher)

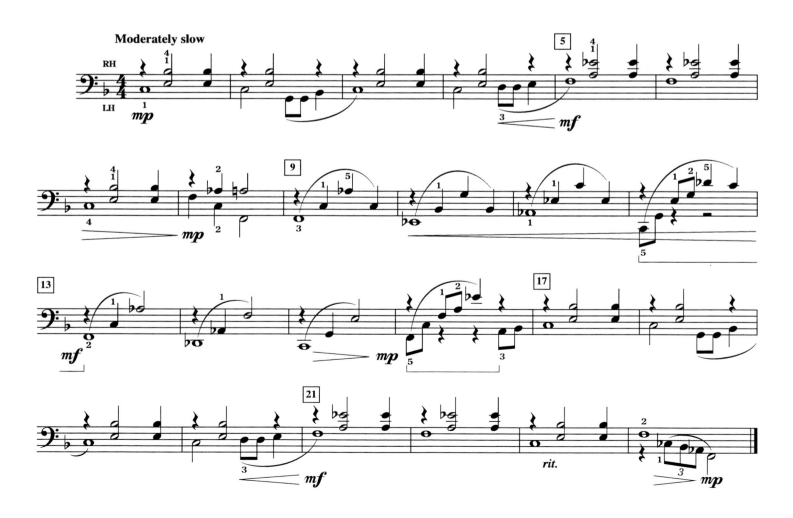

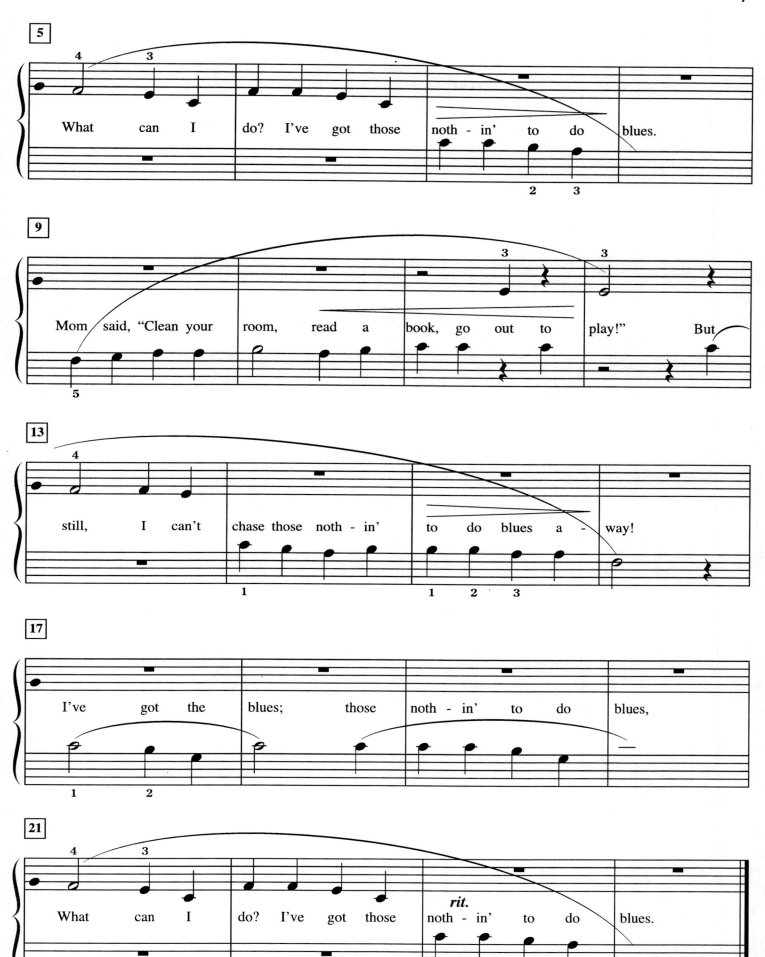

for Katie "Cricket" Mier

Katie Cricket

Martha Mier

Ka - tie Crick - et loves to sing her bright and cheer - y song. When the day - light fades a - way she sings the whole night long. Chirp!

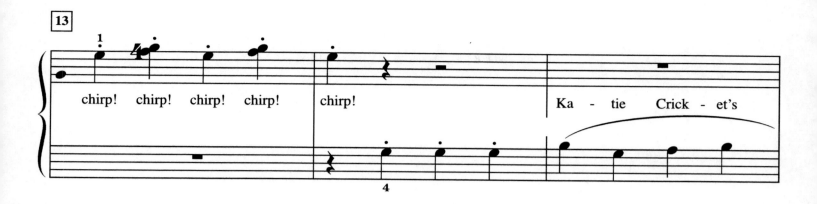

chirp! chirp! chirp! chirp! chirp! Ka - tie Crick - et's

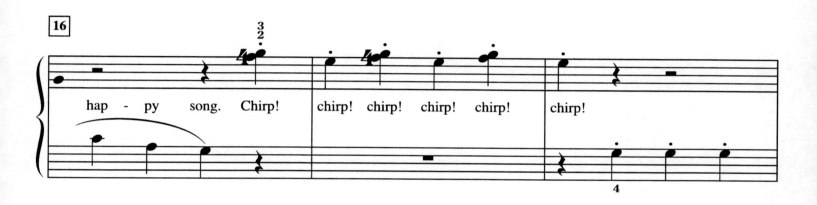

hap - py song. Chirp! chirp! chirp! chirp! chirp! chirp!

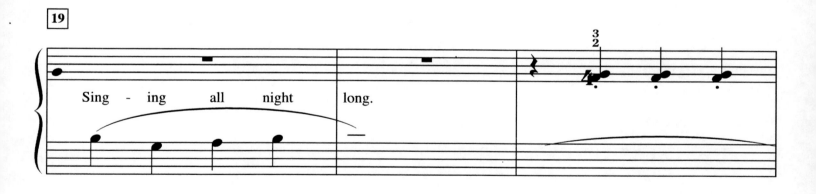

Sing - ing all night long.

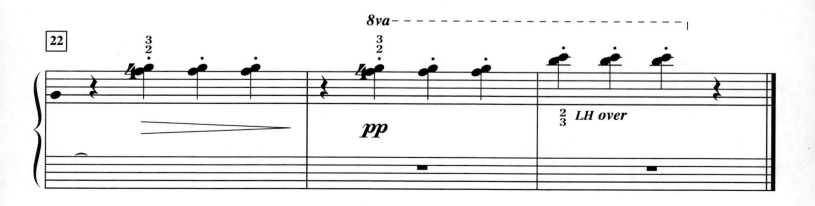

8va -

pp

$\frac{2}{3}$ *LH over*

Charlie's Adventure

Music by Martha Mier
Words by Resha Mier

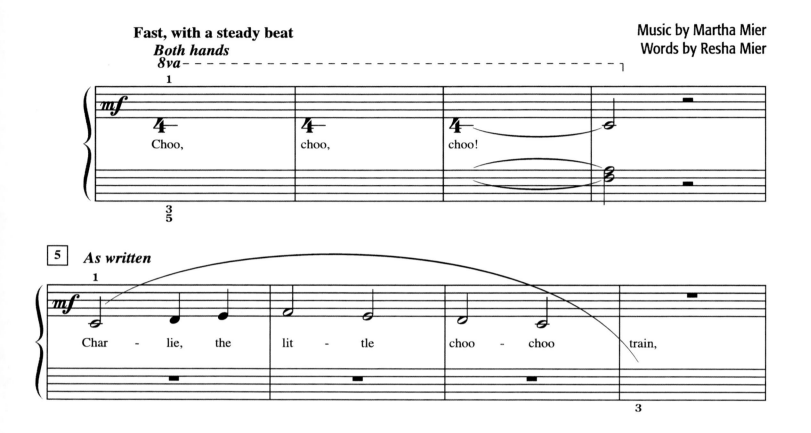

OPTIONAL DUET PART

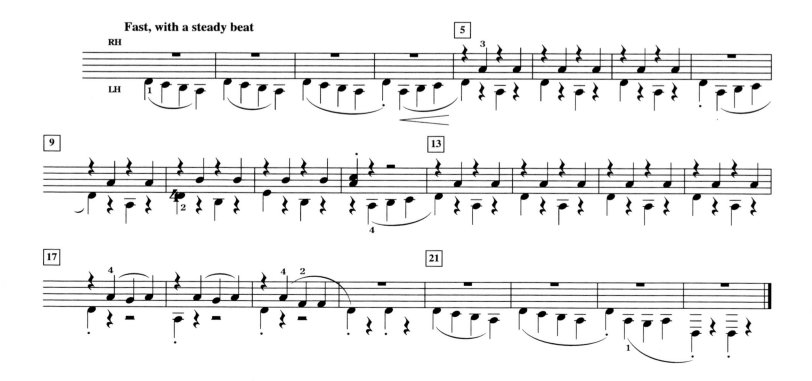

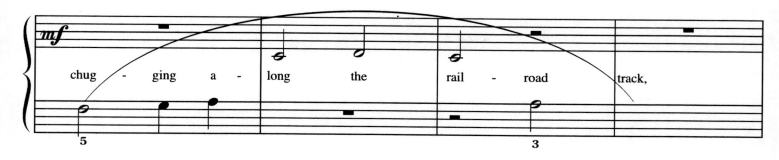

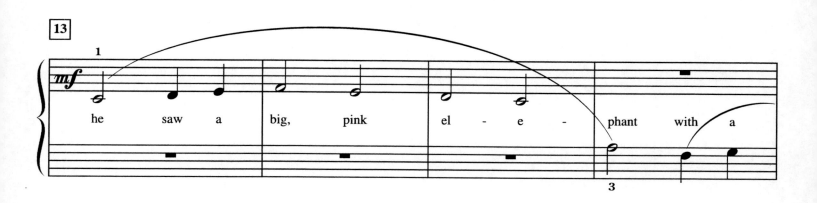

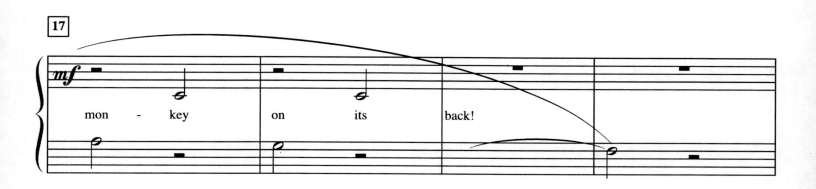

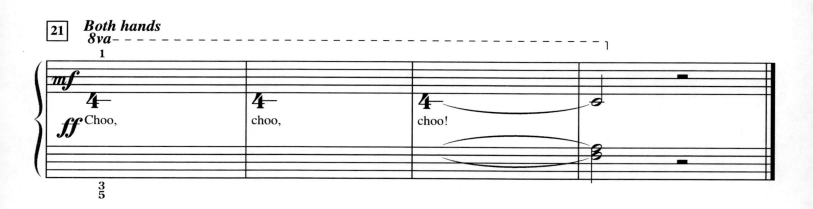

Bumblebee Blues

Martha Mier

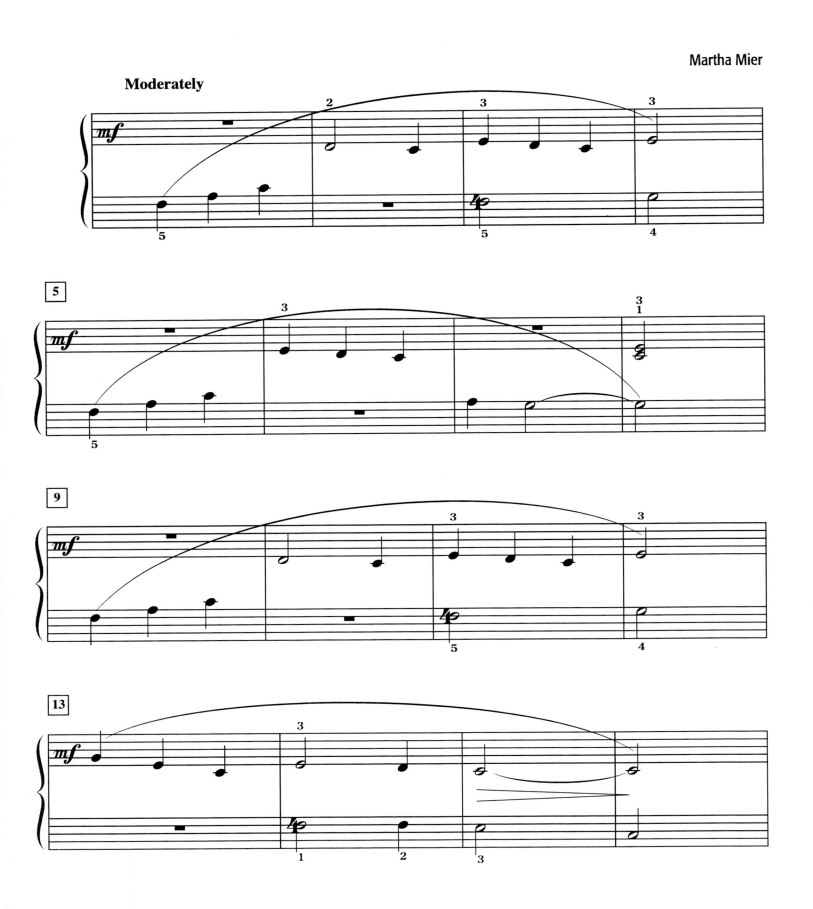

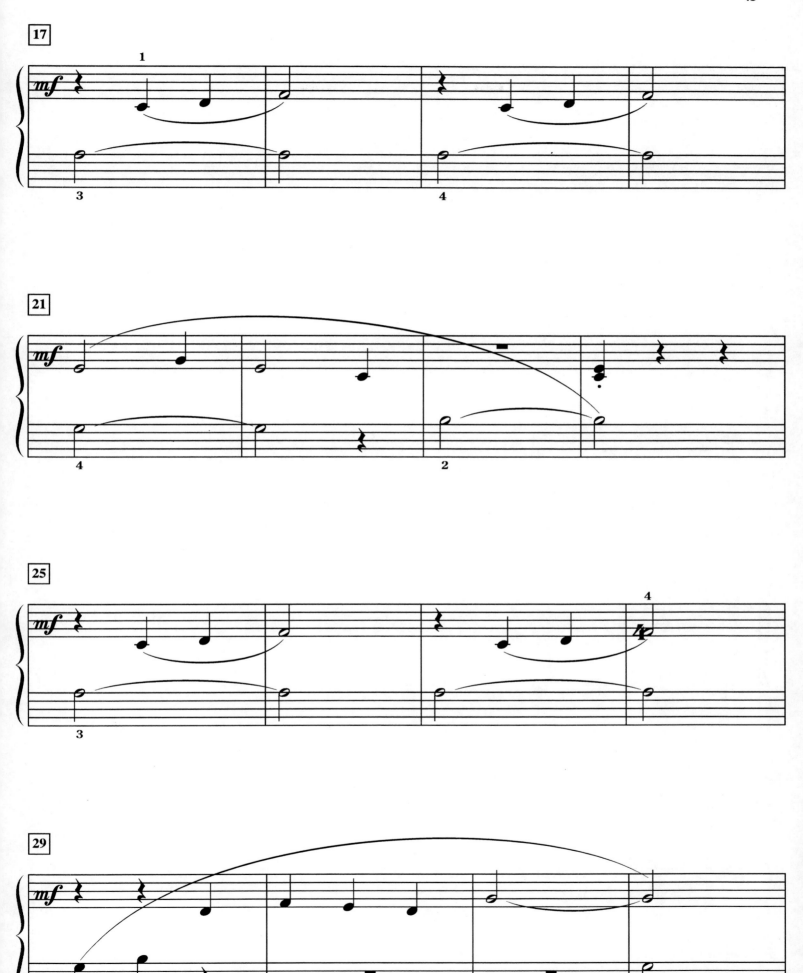

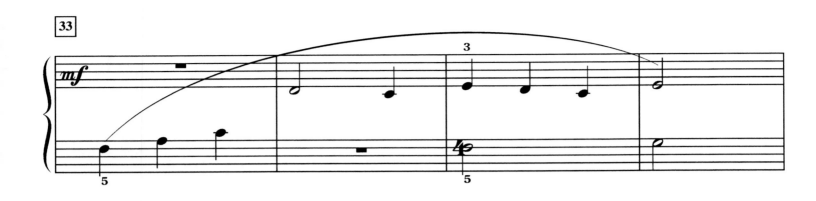

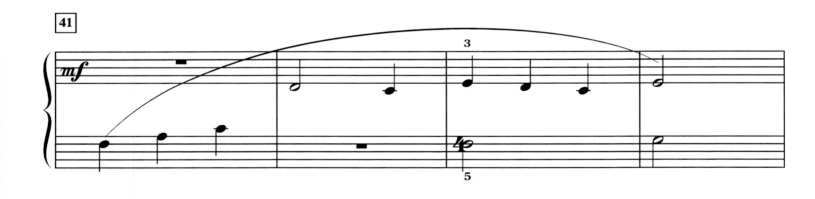

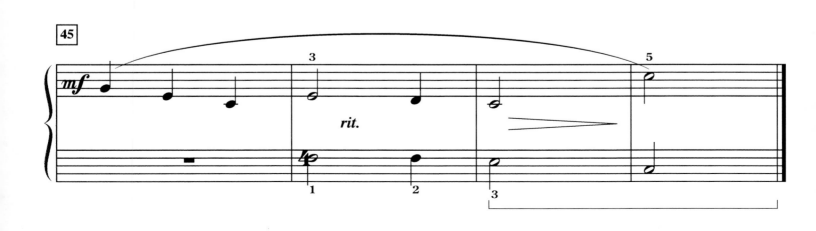

Swingin' and Swayin'

Martha Mier

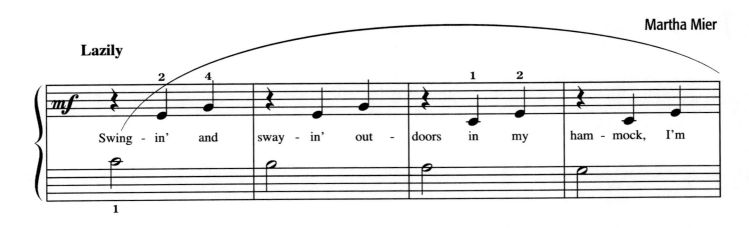

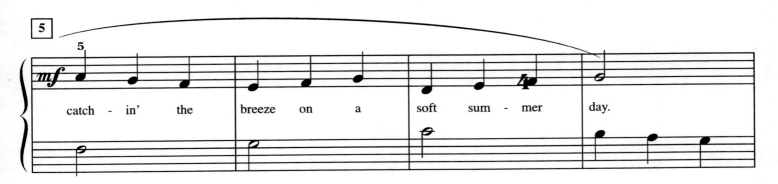

Both hands
8va- -

17

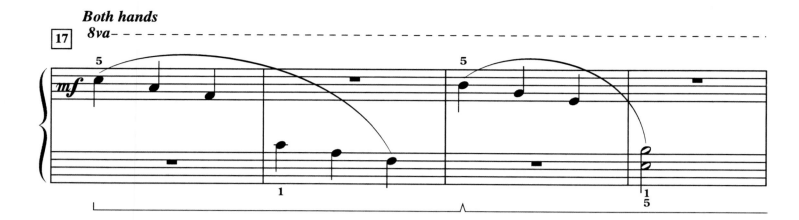

21

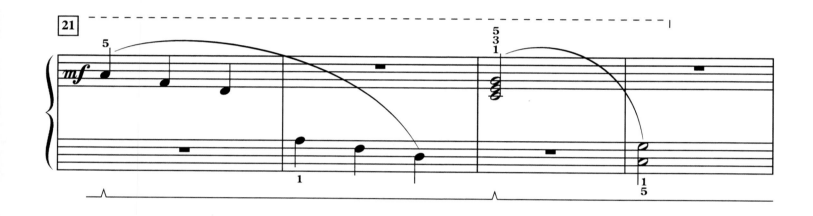

25 *as written*

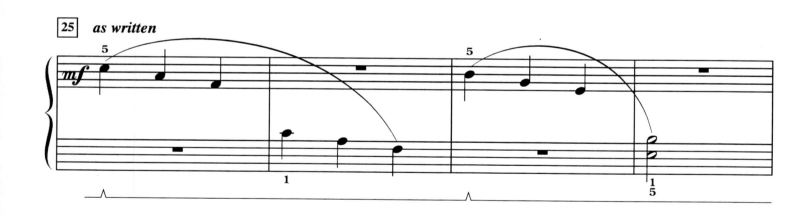

29

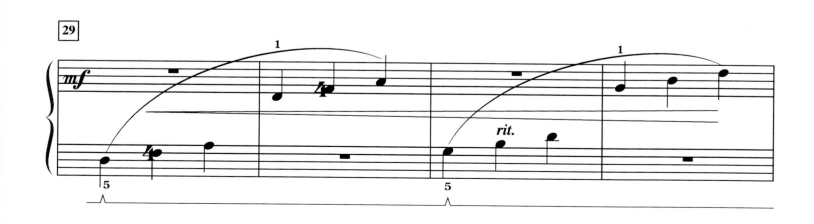

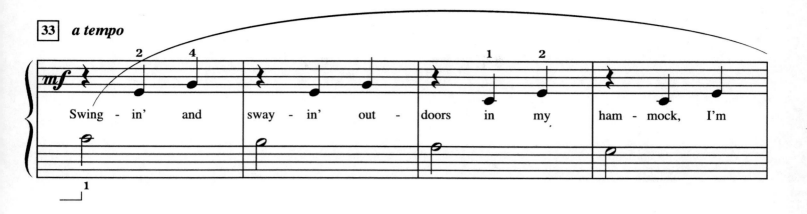

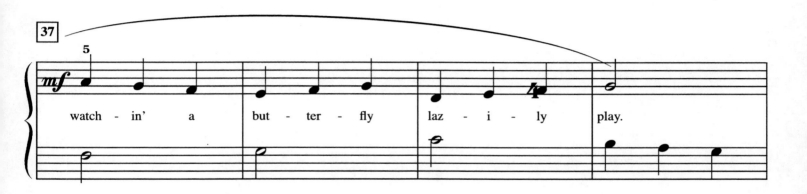

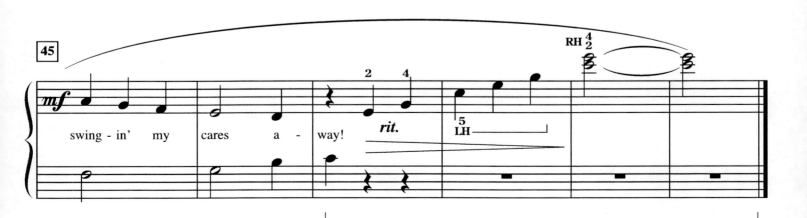

The Hiccup Song

Martha Mier

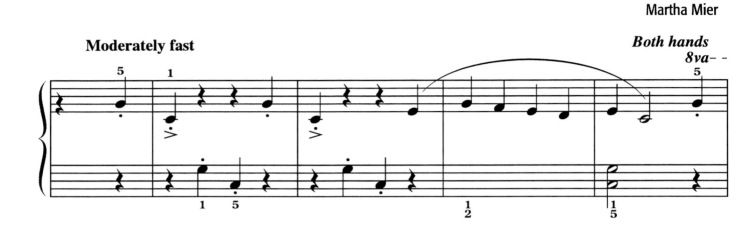

First I held my breath and then I drank a glass of

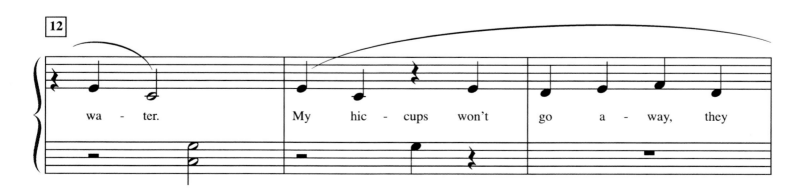

wa - ter. My hic - cups won't go a - way, they

won't do what they ought - er! Hic - cup! (Hic - cup) Hic -

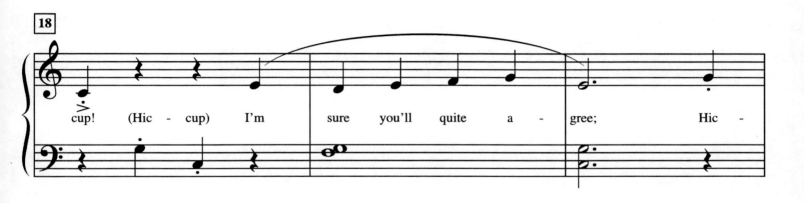

cup! (Hic - cup) I'm sure you'll quite a - gree; Hic -

cup! (Hic - cup) Hic - cup! (Hic - cup) They've got the best of

Very slowly

Both hands 8va- -

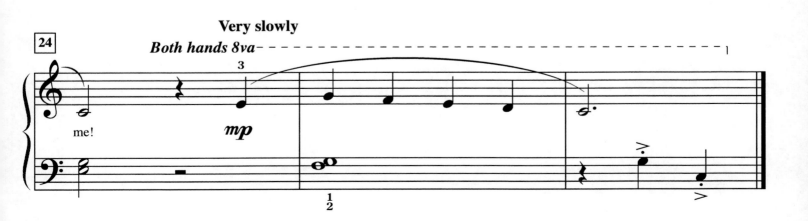

me! *mp*

Frog on a Log

Martha Mier

Moderato

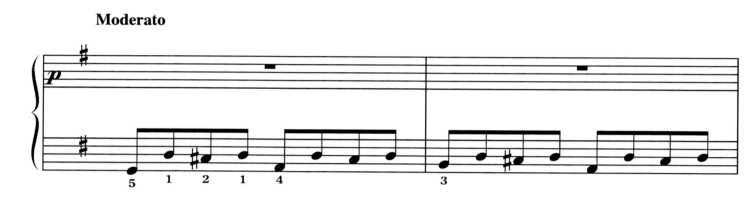

3

Play RH one octave lower
1st time only

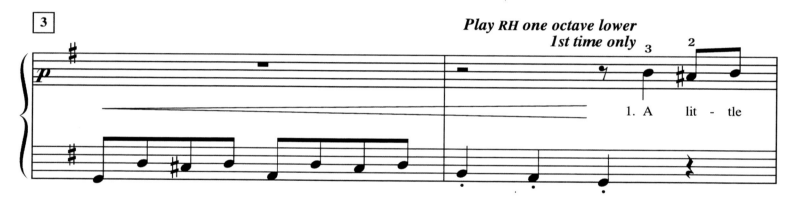

1. A   lit - tle

5

frog   sat   on   a   log;   he   had   his
fly   said, "Me oh   my!   I'll meet my

7

eye   up - on   a   fly.   "That   lit - tle
fate   up - on   his   plate!   I   think I'll

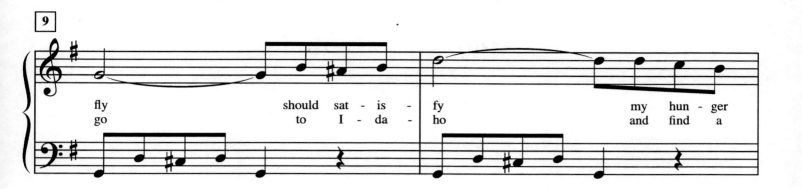

fly
go

should sat - is -
to I - da -

fy
ho

my hun - ger
and find a

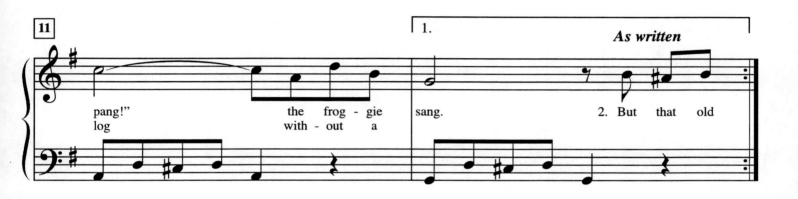

pang!"
log

the frog - gie
with - out a

sang.

As written

2. But that old

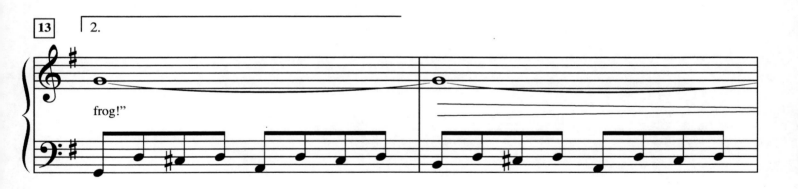

2.

frog!"

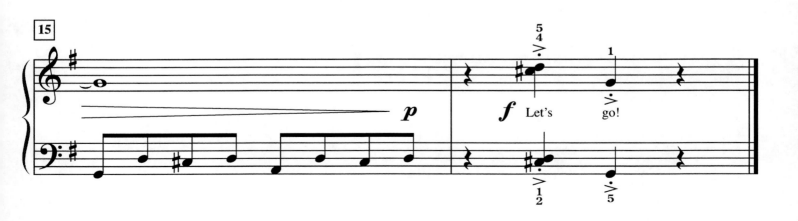

p

f Let's

go!

King of the Jungle

Martha Mier

Li - on in the zoo, when I vis - it you,

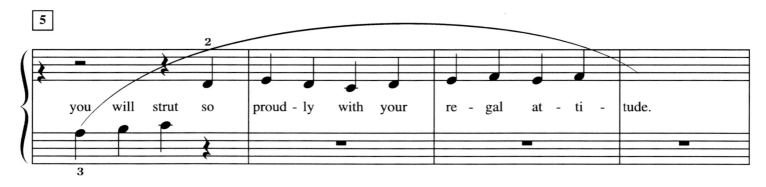

you will strut so proud - ly with your re - gal at - ti - tude.

DUET PART (Student plays 1 octave higher)

With your gold - en mane, you'll stay ev - er - more,

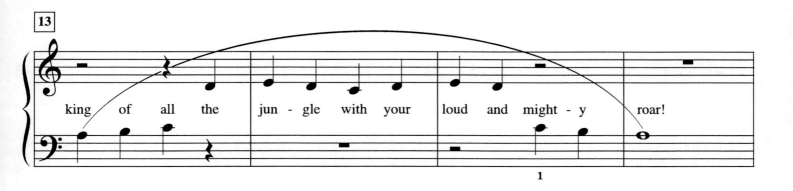

king of all the jun - gle with your loud and might - y roar!

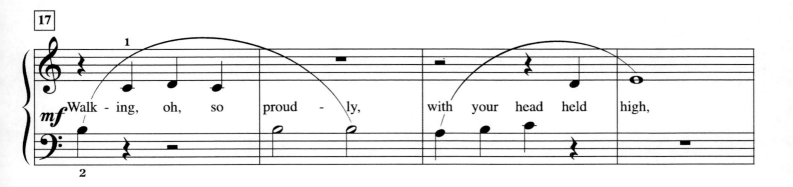

Walk - ing, oh, so proud - ly, with your head held high,

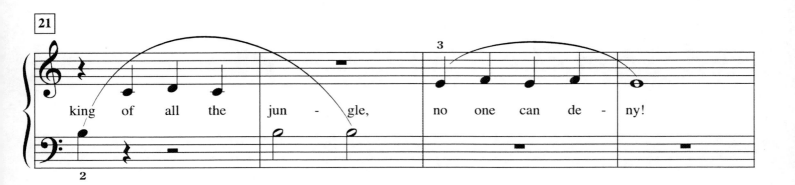

king of all the jun - gle, no one can de - ny!

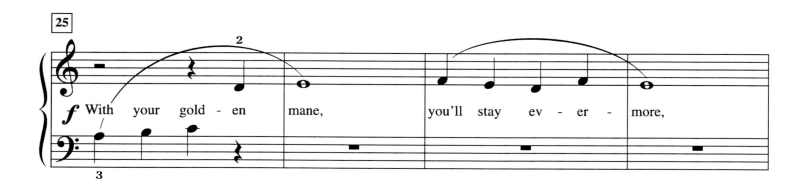

With your gold - en mane, you'll stay ev - er - more,

king of all the jun - gle with your loud and might - y roar!

Press damper pedal and hold

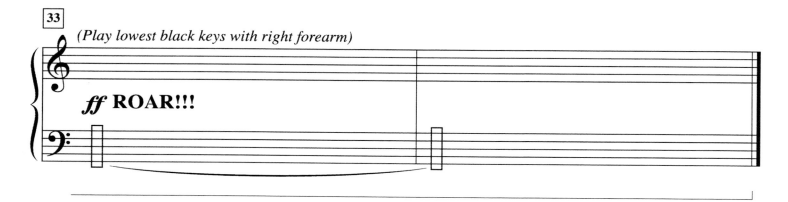

(Play lowest black keys with right forearm)

ff ROAR!!!

DUET PART (Continued)

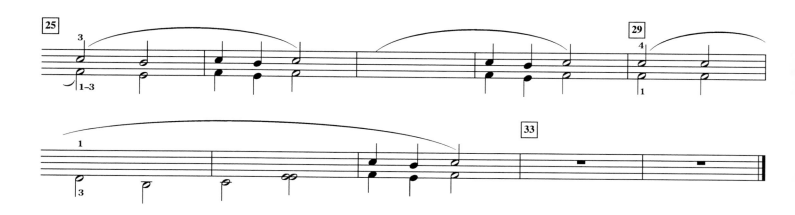